NATURE CLOSE-UP

SPITTLEBUGS
and Other Sap Tappers

TEXT BY ELAINE PASCOE

PHOTOGRAPHS BY DWIGHT KUHN

BLACKBIRCH®
PRESS

THOMSON
GALE

San Diego • Detroit • New York • San Francisco • Cleveland • New Haven, Conn. • Waterville, Maine • London • Munich

For more information, contact
The Gale Group, Inc.
27500 Drake Rd.
Farmington Hills, MI 48331-3535
Or you can visit our Internet site at http://www.gale.com

Photo Credits: All pages © Dwight R. Kuhn Photography

LIBRARY OF CONGRESS CATALOGING-IN-PUBLICATION DATA

Pascoe, Elaine.
  Spittlebugs / by Elaine Pascoe.
      p. cm. — (Nature close up)
Summary: Investigates the physical characteristics, reproductive processes, habitats, and other traits of spittlebugs, aphids, and other members of the Homoptera family. Includes activities.
Includes bibliographical references (p. 47).
  ISBN 1-56711-430-X (hardback : alk. paper)
  1. Cercopidae—Juvenile literature. [1. Spittle insects. 2. Insects—Experiments. 3. Experiments.] I. Title.

QL527.C4 P37 2003
595.7'52—dc21   2002015881

Printed in China
10 9 8 7 6 5 4 3 2 1

CONTENTS

1

The Sap Tappers

Walking through tall grass, you feel something cool and wet brush against your leg. There, sticking to a plant stem, is a gross, foamy glob of . . . could that be spit?

Take a closer look. This "spit" isn't what it seems. The foam is made by an insect called a spittlebug. Inside the blob, a tiny young spittlebug is hiding. It has tapped into the plant stalk and is busily drinking the plant's sap.

Spittlebugs belong to a big group of fascinating insects. Scientists call this group **Homoptera**.

The spittlebug surrounds itself with a blob of foamy bubbles.

There are more than 32,000 different kinds of insects in this group, and they are found worldwide. Among them are tiny whiteflies, which are barely 0.06 inch (1.5 mm) long, and huge tropical cicadas that grow up to 3 inches (76 mm) long. Other common Homoptera members include aphids, leafhoppers, planthoppers, and scale insects. Like the spittlebug, all these insects feed by sucking juices from plants. Some of them do serious damage to crops and gardens.

Left: Spittlebug froth on a plant stem

Right: A periodical cicada

6

One Big Family

Members of the Homoptera group share many traits. Like all insects, they have six legs and three body segments—head, thorax, and abdomen. They also have a hard outer covering called an **exoskeleton**, instead of an internal bony skeleton like yours. Most of the sap tappers are green or brown, so they blend in with the plants on which they live. This helps them hide from predators.

Aphids cluster on a plant stem, sucking juices.

An aphid uses its sharp beak, or proboscis, to pierce a plant stem.

As adults, many members of this insect group have two pairs of wings. When they are at rest, the front wings are generally folded up over the back, so they look like a little tent or a peaked roof. Antennae, which let the insect feel and taste the world around it, may be thin or bristly, like bottlebrushes.

To feed, the insect pierces the outer wall of a stem or leaf with its short, sharp beak, called a **proboscis**. Then it sucks up the juices inside. A special structure in the insect's digestive system filters the sap, and the insect absorbs sugars and other nutrients it needs. Many of these insects use only a small part of the sap they take in. The rest is excreted as a clear, sugary substance called **honeydew**. When lots of the insects are feeding in a tree, a sticky glaze of honeydew may build up on outdoor furniture, cars, and anything else that's underneath.

Most sap tappers have three life stages: egg, **nymph**, and adult. Females lay their eggs on plants. The eggs stay on the plant during the winter, and in spring they hatch into nymphs. The nymphs do not have wings. They crawl around the plant, feeding on sap and growing. As they grow, they molt, or shed their skin, several times. Finally, the insect molts one last time and emerges as a winged adult.

Some sap tappers don't follow this life cycle precisely. That's just one of the ways in which members of this insect group differ from one another.

Left: A planthopper egg

Opposite, left: A planthopper nymph. It is nearly mature and has wing pads, where wings will form later.

Opposite, right: A winged planthopper adult

11

The scarlet and green leafhopper will hop, run, jump, or fly when disturbed.

12

HOPPERS

Scientists divide the sap tapper insects into sub-groups based on physical traits. *Leafhoppers* make up the biggest subgroup. There are more than 2,500 different kinds of leafhoppers in the United States and Canada. They are small insects, ranging from about $\frac{1}{10}$ inch to $\frac{1}{2}$ inch (3 to 12 mm) long, with narrow, wedge-shaped bodies. Leafhoppers are very active—they can hop, jump, run sideways, or fly when disturbed. Different kinds of leafhoppers prefer different host plants, and some are major crop pests.

The *treehoppers* are an odd-looking gang. These small insects have a knobby covering that projects over the body. The covering is shaped and colored to make the insect look like a thorn or a small twig. Tropical treehoppers are the wildest of this group, with their weird spines, hooks, and barbs. In North America, treehoppers are found on field plants, shrubs, and trees. Their strange shapes help them blend in with their surroundings, hiding them from predators.

A female treehopper lays her eggs on a leaf.

13

A spittlebug nymph makes foam from plant sap.

Many *planthoppers* look a lot like leafhoppers, but some members of this group are wider and shorter, with a curved, hornlike projection on the head. Like leafhoppers and treehoppers, different types of planthoppers feed on different plants. Some types damage citrus and other fruit crops, but as pests, planthoppers don't generally do as much harm as leafhoppers do.

Adult *spittlebugs* are about ¼ inch (6 mm) long and look like leafhoppers with blunt heads and large eyes. They are sometimes called froghoppers because they remind some people of tiny frogs. The nymphs are not as lively as leafhopper nymphs. They prefer to stay put on their plant stems, surrounded by frothy spittle.

An adult spittlebug stays inside its protective foam for a short time.

The spittle is actually excess plant sap, which is mixed with a substance made by glands in the insect's abdomen. As it's excreted, the mixture passes through a pair of hard plates that force air into it. The result is a bubbly froth that the spittlebug nymph pulls over itself. The spittle protects the insect from the sun and from predators. Eventually the nymph changes into a winged adult. It stays in the foam for a short while but then leaves to find a mate.

Singers

Cicadas are the largest members of the Homoptera group. The cicadas common in North America are generally 1 to 2 inches (25 to 50 mm) in length, with long, transparent wings. They are sometimes called locusts, but true locusts belong to a different insect family.

Many scientists agree that cicadas are the noisiest animals in the world. A male cicada makes a loud buzzing sound by vibrating two hard membranes on the sides of its abdomen. The cicada's song is a familiar sound in summer. Sometimes thousands of the insects sing together, and up close the sound can be ear splitting. Some male songs have been measured at 112 decibels, which is almost as loud as a jet engine. The main purpose of the male's song is to attract females.

After mating, the female lays her eggs. She uses a sawlike organ called an **ovipositor**, which extends from her abdomen, to split the bark of twigs and place the eggs under it. When the eggs hatch, the tiny nymphs drop to the ground. They burrow into the soil, where they feed on tree roots. Cicada nymphs spend years in the ground, growing and molting.

This periodical cicada has just left its last nymph skin and become a winged adult.

When the nymph is finally ready, it tunnels to the surface and crawls up a tree trunk. There, it molts and becomes a winged adult. Adults live just 5 to 6 weeks, long enough to mate and begin the cycle again.

Some cicadas take two years to complete this cycle. Others, called periodical cicadas, have 13- or 17-year life cycles. In some places, huge swarms of periodical cicadas crawl out of the ground regularly every 13 or 17 years. It is quite a sight. The mass appearance actually helps the insects survive. There are so many that, even if birds and predators gobble up thousands, many others will survive to breed and lay eggs.

A SWEET DEAL

Aphids, leafhoppers, and many other sap-tapping insects produce honeydew. This clear, sticky substance is full of sugar and other nutrients, and it's a source of food for other animals. Among them are certain ants, which sometimes tend leafhoppers or aphids the way people tend cows. It's a good deal for both species. The ants protect the little insects from predators and may move them to good feeding spots. In exchange, the ants collect the honeydew that the aphids and leafhoppers produce.

Ants collect honeydew from aphids, which ants tend the way people tend cows.

TINY TAPPERS

Aphids are tiny insects—most are no bigger than the head of a pin. They are common on garden plants, where they cluster on stems and under leaves. Some people call these soft-bodied insects plant lice.

There are lots of different kinds of aphids. Most are green, but they may be black, gray, brown, pink, red, yellow, or even lavender. Some species, known as woolly aphids, are covered with threads of a white waxy material they produce from special glands.

Two adult female aphids cluster with their tiny offspring.

19

Aphids suck juices from a milkweed leaf. Some people call these tiny insects plant lice.

20

Several generations of aphids may feed on the same plant.

Adelgids are closely related to aphids. They feed only on conifers, such as hemlock and spruce trees, while aphids feed on many different plants.

Aphids have very complicated life cycles. Typically, they produce several generations in a single summer. The first generation hatches from eggs in spring. These aphids have no wings.

All are females, but they can reproduce asexually—without mating. They soon produce a second generation of wingless females, which are born live. These daughters, in turn, give birth to daughters of their own. Finally, as cold weather nears, winged males as well as females are produced. They mate, and the females lay eggs that hatch the following spring.

Scales and More

Scale insects wear a sort of armor. A hard shell or a thick layer of waxy material, which may be powdery or fuzzy and cottonlike, covers these small insects. The coverings protect them from natural enemies and chemical sprays. Safe inside their coats, the insects hardly move. Females have no wings, and many even lose their legs and antennae when they become adults. They spend their whole lives in one place on a host plant, drinking sap. Males, which are smaller than the females, move around more. They keep their legs, and some have wings.

    Mealybugs are soft scale insects. Their small oval bodies are dusted all over with waxy whitish powder, and threads of the same material often stick out from their sides. *Whiteflies* belong to a different subgroup, but they also have waxy coverings.

Inset: Adult whiteflies have a powdery wax coating.

22

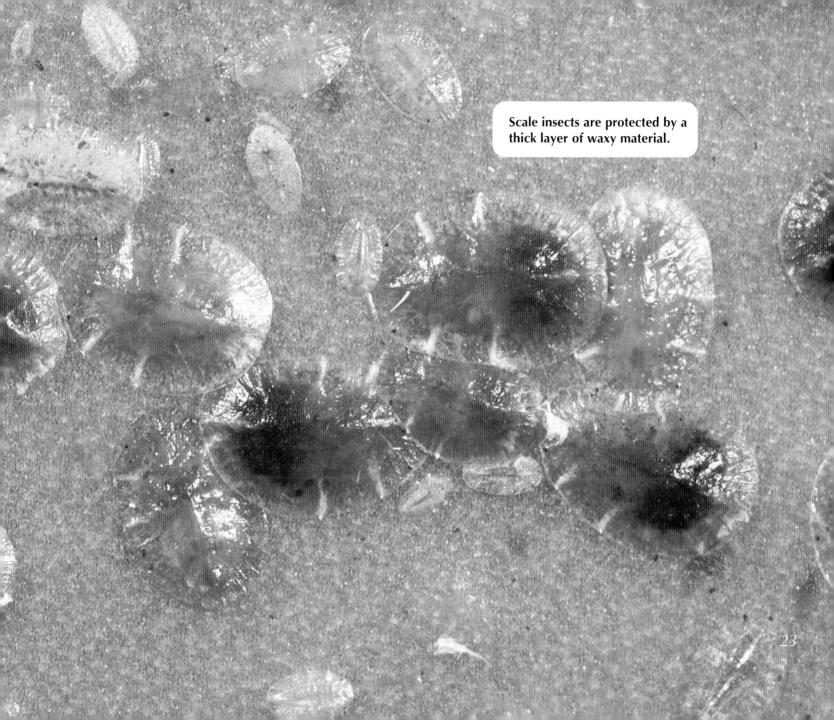

Scale insects are protected by a thick layer of waxy material.

Tiny adult whiteflies have a powdery wax coating on their bodies and wings. The nymphs tap into the undersides of leaves and stay in one spot, like scale insects. *Psyllids* are small, aphidlike insects. Many psyllids are covered with a woolly layer of wax.

The apple psyllid feeds on apple trees.

Helpers or Pests?

Because cicadas go underground for years and then suddenly reappear, people in many cultures have seen them as symbols of rebirth. Long ago in China, jade carvings of cicadas were placed in the mouths of the dead. This was supposed to guarantee immortality for the soul.

In some places, cicadas are considered a gourmet delicacy. People have also found odd uses for some scale insects. A scale insect that lives on cacti is the source of a bright red dye. Another, native to India and Southeast Asia, is the source of natural shellac, which was once widely used on furniture. The shellac insects cluster tightly on fig trees, where their scales form a coating up to $\frac{1}{4}$ inch (6 mm) thick. Although synthetic varnish is more widely used today, the scales are still harvested and processed to make shellac.

Many cultures view cicadas as symbols of rebirth.

Farmers and gardeners, however, are never happy to see sap tappers. Many members of the Homoptera group are major pests. Aphids, leafhoppers, and scale insects damage plants by sucking their juices. Aphids and leafhoppers also spread plant diseases as they move from plant to plant. These insects attack many different crops, as well as garden plants. Whiteflies and mealybugs attack houseplants and greenhouse stock. Adelgids attack evergreen trees, as do pine spittlebugs. These insects are not all harmful, though. Unlike true locusts, cicadas don't eat crops. Meadow spittlebugs leave their unsightly globs in farm fields and gardens, but they rarely do much damage.

26

To gardeners, sap suckers like these rose aphids are pests.

Farmers and gardeners often use chemical sprays to control sap-tapping pests. They can also turn to the insects' natural enemies for help. Insect predators such as lacewings, ladybugs, damsel bugs, mantids, flower flies, and assassin bugs love to gobble up leafhoppers and aphids. Tiny parasitic wasps can also help. These wasps lay their eggs in aphids and some other sap tappers. When the eggs hatch, the wasp larvae feed on the host insect and kill it. By using predators and parasites, people can limit the use of chemicals that harm the environment.

Ladybugs eat aphids and can help control them in gardens.

GALL IN THE FAMILY

A gall is a round growth that sticks out from a tree branch, as if someone had slipped a marble under the bark. These growths are made by insects, including certain aphids.

The growth starts when a female gall aphid starts to feed on a twig. As it sucks up sap, the aphid injects saliva into the twig. The saliva contains a chemical that speeds up the growth of plant tissue. Soon tissue grows around the aphid, forming a gall. The gall is often open at one end, so the insect can get out.

Inside the gall, the aphid gives birth to wingless daughters. Several generations of aphids may develop in the gall during spring and summer. In late summer a generation of winged males and females develops, and leaves the gall to mate and lay eggs.

Sumac galls (left) are each started by a single female aphid (center). Several generations may develop inside the gall (right).

 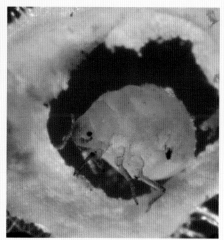 

2

Collecting Flowers
and Caring for Sap Tappers

You won't have to look far to find spittlebugs, aphids, and other sap tappers. Many of these insects are common in fields and gardens, especially in summer. That makes them great subjects for nature study. You can watch the insects feed, and maybe observe parts of their life cycle. A hand lens will help you study aphids and other small insects.

You can also catch some of these insects and keep them for a while, so you can study them close up.

You'll need to provide the insects with a temporary home and some of the plants they feed on. This section will tell you how to do that. When you have finished studying the insects, take them back to the place where you found them and release them. Because many of these insects are considered pests, they should not be released in new areas.

Tomatoes and other garden plants are good places to hunt for sap tappers.

To find aphids, follow the ants that care for them.

Aphid Hunt

Chances are there are aphids in a field or garden near you. But you'll have to look closely to find them. Aphids are so small that they're hard to spot, and they're often colored to blend in with their host plants—the plants where they feed. Rose bushes, lettuce, peas, and milkweed plants are aphid favorites. But some aphids go for other plants. Look around to see which plants they feed on in your area.

By late summer you may find clusters of aphids, adults and offspring.

Check the tips of plant stems and the leaves nearest the tips, which are aphids' favorite feeding places. In early summer you may find only a few aphids, but by late summer there may be large clusters. Ants crawling on a plant stem are a clue that aphids may be present. The ants may be on the plant to collect the honeydew that these insects produce.

If you want to take a few aphids home to study, bring along plant snippers and a jar or plastic container. Cut a stem or branch where aphids are feeding and put it, together with the insects, in the container. Collect some extra stems and leaves from a host plant, too.

Keeping Aphids

At home, put the plant stems in a container, using stones to hold them upright. Add water to keep the plants healthy, but not so much that the stones are completely covered. This way, if aphids fall off the plants, they won't drown. They'll be able to crawl up onto the stones. Aphids tend to stay put, so you may not need to cover the container. If you want, however, you can cover it with mesh and a rubber band.

A glass jar makes a good temporary home for aphids.

34

In a few days, the plants will start to wilt. Aphids won't be able to draw juices from the wilted plants, so you'll need to release the insects. Or you can collect more stems from the same type of plant and transfer the aphids to the fresh stems.

If you want to keep aphids for a long time, dig up a complete host plant, roots and all. Put the plant in a flowerpot with some soil. Don't forget to give the plant water and a good source of light, to keep it healthy.

To keep aphids for a long time, give them a host plant.

Spittlebug Safari

Spittlebugs are easier to spot than aphids. In spring and early summer, look for the foamy spittle these insects make. You'll find the $1/2$- to $3/4$-inch (12 to 18 mm) blobs on the stems of meadow grasses, weeds, and garden plants. Carefully probe the foam with a small stick to see the little nymph inside.

To collect the insect, cut the stem of the plant it's on. Put the plant stem, spittlebug and all, in a container with a small amount of water in the bottom. You can leave the container uncovered or put mesh, secured with a rubber band, over the top.

Push aside the foam on a plant stem, and you'll probably find spittlebug nymphs.

For a better look, you may want to remove the insect from its foam. Lift it out with a small paintbrush and put it in a new place on the plant. The nymph will move around to find a good feeding place and then begin to make more foam.

If the plant begins to wilt, cut another stem from the same type of plant. Put the fresh stem in the container, and transfer the spittlebug to it with a soft paintbrush.

Left: Put a plant stem with spittlebugs in a container with water.
Above: You can cover the container with mesh to make sure the insects don't get out.

Investigating Sap Tappers

In this section, you'll find some projects and activities that will help you learn more about spittlebugs and their relatives, and about the ways these insects affect their host plants. Some of these activities can be done with insects in the wild, and some with insects that you collect. Have fun with these activities. When you're done, remember to return any insects you've collected to the places where you found them.

WHAT HAPPENS TO A PLANT THAT'S CROWDED WITH APHIDS?

Do you know why gardeners hate aphids? Based on what you've read, make a guess about how aphids affect plants. Then find out if you're right by doing this activity, using plants and insects in the wild. Try to use weeds, such as milkweed. If you use garden plants, be sure to check with the gardener first.

What You Need:
* 3 plants of the same type and condition, all hosting aphids
* Small paintbrush

What to Do:

1. Use your paintbrush to remove all the aphids from one plant. Keep this plant aphid-free throughout your experiment.
2. Remove most of the aphids from the second plant. Keep the number of aphids on this plant low.
3. Leave the aphids on the third plant alone, so they can multiply unchecked.
4. Check the plants every day. Look for changes in their appearance, and keep a record of your observations.

Results: Compare the three plants, noting their growth and any signs of poor health, such as wilting stems or yellowed leaves.

Conclusion: How did the condition of each plant change over time? Did the plant crowded with aphids show changes that the other plants did not?

WHAT WILL APHIDS DO IF YOU CUT A STEM WHERE THEY ARE FEEDING?

Aphids seem to like to cluster near the tips of stems and branches. What will happen if the stem is cut below their feeding place? Decide what you think, and then do this activity to see if you are right. If you use garden plants, check with the gardener first.

What You Need:
* 2 plants of the same type, both hosting aphids
* Scissors or plant snippers
* Clothespin

What to Do:

1. On one plant, locate a stem where aphids are feeding. Cut this stem below the aphids' feeding place. Leave the second plant uncut.

2. Use the clothespin to attach the cut stem from the first plant to the second plant.

3. Check the plant every day.

Results: After several days, note how many aphids remain on the cut stem and on the uncut plant.

Conclusions: What happened to the aphids on the cut stem? Can you think of a reason for the outcome?

WHAT HAPPENS IF YOU MOVE APHIDS TO A DIFFERENT KIND OF PLANT?

Aphids are found on many different kinds of plants. But will an aphid from a milkweed, for example, be happy on a rose? Decide what you think, based on what you know about these insects. Then find out by doing this activity.

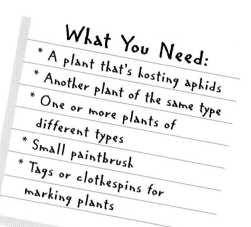

What You Need:
* A plant that's hosting aphids
* Another plant of the same type
* One or more plants of different types
* Small paintbrush
* Tags or clothespins for marking plants

What to Do:

1. Using your paintbrush, move some aphids from the host plant to nearby plants of different types. You can also do this experiment with cuttings and insects you've collected.
2. Also move some aphids to a plant of the same type as the host plant.
3. Check the plants for aphids every day.

Results: Note which plants still have aphids.

Conclusions: Did aphids stay on plants where they weren't found? If not, did the type of plant or the fact that you moved them cause them to leave? Try the experiment again, using other types of plants. Are the results different?

HOW QUICKLY CAN A SPITTLEBUG COVER ITSELF WITH FOAM?

Spittlebugs produce their foam by forcing air into excess plant sap that they have sucked in. Just how good are they at blowing bubbles? Guess how long it will take one of these little insects to cover itself with foam, and then do this activity. You can use spittlebugs in a field or insects that you've collected.

What to Do:

1. Using the paintbrush, gently lift a spittlebug out of its foam. Then place it back on the same plant.
2. Watch the insect. It will probably wander around for a while, looking for a good place to feed. Then it will settle in and begin to make foam.

Results: Time the insect from the start of its foam making to the point where it's completely covered. If you can, repeat the activity using different spittlebugs.

Conclusion: How long did the spittlebugs take to cover themselves? Were some faster than others? What factors might have led to different times?

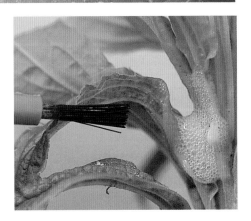

Do Spittlebugs Prefer Certain Plants?

Are spittlebugs happy on a range of plants, or are they picky sap tappers who prefer only one kind? Decide what you think, and then find out with this experiment. To collect the insects and set up a container for them, follow the instructions in Chapter 2.

What You Need:
* Spittlebug nymphs, with the plant stems they were found on
* Stalks of at least 2 other kinds of plants, found nearby
* Small paintbrush
* Spittlebug container (see Chapter 2)

What to Do:

1. Put at least one spittlebug on each type of plant. Use the paintbrush to gently lift the nymph out of its foam and place it on the new stalk.

2. Put all the plants in the spittlebug container, with their stems in water as shown in Chapter 2.

3. Check over time to see where the insects settle.

Results: Note how many spittlebugs end up on each type of plant.

Conclusion: What do your results tell you about spittlebugs' plant preferences? Try the experiment again, using other kinds of plants. Are the results different?

MORE ACTIVITIES WITH SAP TAPPERS

1. Collect an adult aphid and a host plant as described in Chapter 2. Watch the insect over time, providing fresh plants as needed. How long does the aphid take to find a place to feed on the plant? Use a hand lens to examine the insect's body and see how it feeds. Watch to see if it gives birth to a daughter. How long does the birth take? How many daughters does the aphid produce over five days?

2. Find out how many aphids a ladybug can eat in a day. Collect aphids and place them in a container with a plant stem, as described in Chapter 2. Count the aphids. Then collect a ladybug and put it in the aphid container. Watch what the ladybug does. A day later, count the aphids again. How many are left? Remember to release the ladybug.

An adult female aphid gives birth to a daughter.

3. Watch ants care for aphids. Find a plant that has ants and aphids on it, and observe the insects. Touch the aphids with a small paintbrush. What do the ants do?

4. Look for aphids that have been attacked by parasitic wasps. These aphids are usually fat and either dull tan or brown. Put the aphids in a container and watch to see what happens. (The photo on this page shows one of the wasps emerging from the shell of an aphid.)

5. Take a spittlebug survey. Late spring and early summer are good times for this activity. Find a field with lots of these insects. How many do you see? What kinds of plants are they living on?

Wasp emerging from the shell of the aphid.

Results and Conclusions

Here are some possible results for the activities on pages 38 to 43. Many factors may affect the results of these activities. If your results differ, try to think of reasons why. Repeat the activity with different conditions, and see if your results change.

What Happens to a Plant That's Crowded with Aphids?

A few aphids generally cause no harm. But when a plant is crowded with aphids, you can expect its leaves to curl and turn yellow. This happens because aphids are sucking too much of the plant's juices. The plant's growth may be stunted, and it may even die.

What Will Aphids Do If You Cut a Stem Where They Are Feeding?

After a few days, the cut stem will be wilted. Aphids that were feeding on it will most likely have left or died. They need a constant supply of plant juices, and cutting the stem interrupts the flow of juices up to that part of the plant.

What Happens If You Move Aphids to a Different Kind of Plant?

Aphids moved to plants where they don't normally feed usually leave quickly. Most aphids are very picky about the plants where they feed.

How Quickly Can a Spittlebug Cover Itself with Foam?

Spittlebugs are speedy foam makers—some kinds turn out as many as 80 bubbles per minute. The speed of your spittlebugs will depend on many factors, including the species and age of the nymph and the temperature and humidity of the air.

Do Spittlebugs Prefer Certain Plants?

Your spittlebugs may move back to the plants where they were found. They may also accept some other plants, but reject others. These insects can survive on a range of plants, but they have taste preferences—just as you do.

Some Words About Spittlebugs and Other Sap Tappers

exoskeleton The hard outer skin of an insect. It takes the place of an internal skeleton.

Homoptera The scientific name of a group of insects that feed by sucking plant sap.

honeydew A clear, sugary substance produced by many sap-tapping insects.

nymph An immature form of certain insects. Nymphs often look like adults without wings.

ovipositor An organ that female insects use to lay eggs.

proboscis A sharp beak that sap-tapping insects use to pierce the outer skin of plants.

For More Information

Books

Clyne, Densey. *Cicada Sing-Song.* Gareth Stevens, 2001.

Discovery Channel Science. *Insects.* Gareth Stevens, 2002.

Kneidel, Sally Stenhouse. *Creepy Crawlies and the Scientific Method: More than 100 Hands-On Science Experiments for Children.* Fulcrum Publishing, 1993.

Kneidel, Sally Stenhouse. *Pet Bugs: A Kid's Guide to Catching and Keeping Touchable Insects.* John Wiley & Sons, 1994.

Miller, Sara Swan. *Cicadas and Aphids: What They Have in Common (Animals in Order Series).* Franklin Watts, 1999.

Web sites

BugBios

Find out more about Homoptera — **www.insects.org**

Wonderful World of Insects

Read about cicadas and lots of other insects — **http://www.earthlife.net/insects/six.html**

INDEX